Original title:
Tropical Taste

Copyright © 2025 Creative Arts Management OÜ
All rights reserved.

Author: Olivia Sterling
ISBN HARDBACK: 978-1-80586-241-3
ISBN PAPERBACK: 978-1-80586-713-5

Lush Paradise

In a land where pineapples dance,
Mangoes giggle in a bright romance.
Coconuts wear little grass skirts,
While the sun throws parties, making flirts.

Limes tease lemons in a zesty duel,
Avocados stroll, keeping it cool.
Papayas plot with guavas in the shade,
Jokes were shared, and drinks were made.

Vibrant Vistas

At sunrise, the oranges burst with glee,
While grapefruits sing up in the tree.
Berry bands play a vibrant tune,
As watermelons bask under the moon.

Tropical breezes bring giggles galore,
Lemons jump in, adding zest to the score.
Every fruit seems to wear a grin,
In this fruity fiesta, we all jump in!

A Symphony of Flavors

A serenade of flavors in the air,
Bananas chuckle without a care.
Pineapple plays the ukulele fine,
While cherries dance in a fruity line.

Passions ignite with every sweet bite,
Oranges rolling, what a sight!
The melody of laughter fills the space,
As we all join this lively race.

Breeze and Bananas

Bananas swing in the gentle breeze,
As mangoes whisper secrets through the trees.
Tangerines tumble, laughing out loud,
While the whole fruit bunch forms a crowd.

Coconuts giggle, playing tricks,
Limes throw in some zesty flicks.
The sun winks down, joining the spree,
In this nutty world, we all feel free!

The Color of Papaya

In the kitchen, bright and bold,
A papaya's tale of colors told.
Orange like sunset on a clear day,
Slice it open, watch the fun play.

With seeds like gems, a treasure worth,
Who knew fruit could cause such mirth?
Spoon it out, let laughter fly,
Eating papaya? Oh my, oh my!

Sweet Serenade of Fruits

Bananas dance, all yellow with glee,
Mangoes hum sweet songs under the tree.
Pineapples grin, spiky yet neat,
Making fruit salads a delightful treat.

Kiwis and berries in a fruit fight,
Splashing juice in the morning light.
A symphony of sweetness plays,
Enjoying nature's funny craze!

Coconut Currents

A coconut rolls, round like a ball,
Hiding its water, oh what a wall!
Knock it twice, hear the echo chime,
Is it a drink or just a prank, oh so prime?

With a straw sticking out, like a silly hat,
Sipping the juice, "How sweet is that?"
The shell's a stage for a goofy joke,
In a coconut world, all laugh till they choke!

Ocean's Palette

The sea splashes shades, vibrant and bright,
With fruits from the land, a colorful sight.
Watermelons wave from sandy shore,
While seashells giggle and laugh, wanting more.

Fruits in a tide, they bounce and play,
Mango waves crash, splashing away.
With each fruity splash, a joke unfurls,
In this zany world, where laughter swirls!

Garden of Delight

In a garden where giggles grow,
Mango trees dance, putting on a show.
Bananas slip with a funny flair,
While lemon drops bounce without a care.

Pineapples wear hats, oh what a sight,
Coconut dreams take flight at night.
Jokes sprout with each playful vine,
In this land where flavors intertwine.

Papayas chuckle, their faces round,
In this joyful patch, laughter abounds.
Bees buzz along to the fruity tune,
Under the sun, dancing with the moon.

So grab a slice of this silly pie,
Where fruit is king, and joy floats high.
In this garden, let your spirits lift,
A fruity wonderland, nature's gift.

Coral Reefs and Citrus

Underwater laughs in the coral spree,
Fish wear sunglasses, sipping iced tea.
Lemons surf on waves, a zesty crew,
While grapefruits float, acting brand new.

With seaweed hats and shells in tow,
They dance in the current, putting on a show.
Starfish giggle, their jokes offbeat,
As citrus slices share cool treats.

Crabs wear bibs for the juicy feast,
With every bite, they laugh the least.
Oranges rolling in the ocean foam,
Make everyone feel right at home.

Invite your friends for a splashy time,
Where lemon-lime waves create a rhyme.
In this coral cove, joy prevails,
Where laughter rides on citrus gales.

Sun-Kissed Flavors

Beneath the rays where the bananas grin,
A watermelon dives with a splashy spin.
Passion fruit sings with a comical beat,
As cherry tomatoes find their seat.

Grinning peaches roll down the hill,
Munching on laughter, what a thrill!
Sunshine beams like a cheeky prank,
As berries bounce in a fruity tank.

Avocados giggle, going green with glee,
Making guacamole for a fruity spree.
Cucumbers wear shades, feeling so cool,
Mixing with humor, they rule the pool.

So join the party in the sun's warm glow,
With flavors that dance and merriment flows.
In this vibrant place where smiles are found,
Sun-kissed moments are magic unbound.

Citrus Serenade

In the orchard of chuckles where citrus thrive,
Oranges play music to feel alive.
Lime slices swing, twirling with zest,
While grapefruit giggles, taking a rest.

The tangerines wear shoes that squeak,
In a dance-off that's truly unique.
With lemon jokes that never fall flat,
They gather around for a fruity chat.

Citrus serenade, bright on the scene,
Where each little citrus plays like a dream.
Jokes pop like bubbles, full of delight,
In this zesty realm, love takes flight.

So tap your feet to the fruity rhyme,
Where laughter blooms, dancing in time.
A melody of flavors, vintage and new,
In the citrus ball, we're all invited too.

Aroma of the Jungle

In the jungle, fruits swing high,
Bananas wear hats, oh my!
Coconuts giggle as they fall,
Mangoes, ripe, they love to sprawl.

Parrots squawk, they dance and play,
While lizards sip the juice all day.
Papayas in pajamas, bright and bold,
Tickling the taste buds, so manifold.

Rhythms of Rainforest

Beating drums in leafy halls,
Fruit flies groove while the monkey calls.
The rhythm of the forest, quite a sight,
Watermelons roll with sheer delight.

Limes do tango, lemons prance,
In this symphony of a juicy dance.
Bouncing berries scatter their cheer,
While ribbiting frogs join the atmosphere.

Juicy Delights

Grapefruits wearing shades so cool,
Do a hula in the school.
Kiwi with a wink, so proud,
Making jokes that are loud and loud.

Oranges juggling, such a craze,
While squishy guavas start to blaze.
A splash of spice, a hint of fun,
In the fruit parade, we all run!

Dancing Pineapples

Pineapples twirl in crazy shoes,
Bop to the beat, no time to snooze.
With crowns on their heads, they sway and spin,
A fruity fiesta, let the fun begin!

Coconuts clap with a bang and plop,
Giggling berries, they just won't stop.
Dancing at dusk with a twinkling star,
In this zesty universe, we are!

Maracuja Melody

In a grove where fruits collide,
Maracuja sings with pride.
A zesty twist, a cheeky grin,
Dancing peels, let the fun begin!

Juice drips down, a sticky feat,
Bouncing off my wobbly seat.
Taste the splash of golden cheer,
Is that a monkey laughing near?

A Splash of Paradise

In a bowl of sunny cheer,
Papaya giggles, oh so near.
With mangoes dancing in a rush,
They take the stage and make us blush!

A coconut shell, I wear as hat,
Embracing the chaos, how about that?
While pineapples take a silly slide,
We all just laugh, no place to hide!

Passionfruit Daydream

Through the vines, a curious buzz,
Passionfruit whispers, 'What's the fuss?'
Inside, a tangy, squishy surprise,
Oh look, a fruit flies by with style!

Bright yellow seeds, a playful game,
Messy faces, it's never the same.
We scoop and laugh, a fruity spree,
Who knew snacks could be so free?

Swaying Palm Sensations

Beneath the palms, a party brews,
Fruits in hand, we shake our shoes.
Bananas slip, the laughter grows,
It's a slippery path to fruity shows!

With coconuts rolling, we play tag,
"Catch me if you can!"—a fruity brag.
Murmurs of laughter fill the air,
What a wild ride, without a care!

Juices of Joy

In a blender, fruits collide,
Bouncing like a joyful ride.
Mango whispers, 'Take a sip!',
Papaya laughs and does a flip.

Coconuts fall with a loud thud,
One rolls away, it's a nutty flood!
Pineapples giggle, sweet and bright,
Sipping juices feels so right!

Balsam Sea Breeze

Waves crash while the pineapples sway,
Lemons giggle as they play.
Mint leaves tease with a breezy whiff,
Citrus jokes give a happy lift.

The coconuts craft a comedy show,
With lime and salt ready to go.
The sea breeze chuckles, sipping along,
In this zesty world, we belong!

Sweet Serengeti

Beneath a tree, the fruits convene,
Bananas dance in a lively scene.
Mangoes boast of their sweet delight,
Pomegranates join, ready to bite.

The toucan jokes, 'What's your rep?'
The fruits all laugh and take a step.
Out in the sun, there's plenty to share,
A fruity fiesta, without a care!

Picnic by the Palms

Under palms, we spread our spread,
Lying on blankets, dreams ahead.
Watermelons splash with juicy cheer,
While little ants are marching near.

A coconut rolls, making a fuss,
Avocados grin, "Join us, discuss!"
The laughter bubbles, bright like the sun,
In this picnic, we've all won!

Essence of the Tropics

Coconut bra, a dance so free,
Palm trees sway, oh look at me!
Mangoes rolling down the lane,
I slipped and fell, guess I'm in pain!

Pineapple hats, they're quite the craze,
Sippin' rum in a fruity daze.
The sun is bright, the laughter loud,
In this madness, I feel quite proud!

Coastal Canopy

Undersea shades, a fish parade,
With jelly legs, the beach I've laid.
Seagulls squawking in fowl delight,
As I chase crabs, well, isn't that bright?

Sandy toes and coconut drinks,
Hiccups arise as everyone winks.
The piña colada spills on my shirt,
Now it's a party, or is it dessert?

Flavorful Footprints

Footprints in the sand, I leave behind,
A trail of laughter, what did I find?
Bananas slipping, that's my fate,
Rolling down hills, oh isn't that great?

In the market, a fruit fight ensues,
Mango grenades, oh what a ruse!
The papaya flies, I dodge with flair,
Now I'm covered, but I just don't care!

Exotic Elixirs

Melon concoctions in my cup,
A splash of laughter as I sup.
Watermelon hats are all the style,
Join my ridiculous fruit parade, stay awhile!

Fruit punch parties with silly straws,
Lime retreats and guava applause.
With every sip, the giggles rise,
In this fruity game, let's claim the prize!

Maracuja Melodies

In the jungle, fruits giggle,
Maracuja sings a silly wiggle.
With a twisty straw, we slurp and slosh,
A burst of flavor, oh what a bosh!

Limes are laughing, lemons cheer,
Mangoes dance, oh so near.
Coconut smirks in its brown shell,
Beneath the palm tree, who can tell?

Mangrove Morsels

Shrimp in party hats, what a sight,
Dancing with crabs under moonlight.
Baked or grilled, oh, what a tease,
They're schoolyard secrets, if you please!

Seaweed winks from the sandy shore,
As a fish joins the fun, asking for more.
Everyone's laughing, bubbles galore,
Who knew dinner could be such a chore?

Savoring Sunshine

Pineapple hats worn at a fair,
Sipping juice without a care.
A tickle of spice, a dash of sweet,
We dance on the beach with happy feet!

Bananas in pajamas, what a fashion,
Bouncing around with lively passion.
Avocado dives into the fray,
Creating a guac that's here to stay!

Bounty of the Isles

Coconut smiles with a nutty grin,
While mangoes juggle, oh let's begin!
Fruits in a frenzy, all around,
In this wacky world, bliss is found.

Papayas giggle, ripe and round,
As starfruit twirls, joy unbound.
It's a carnival of flavors, so bright,
In this island playground, pure delight!

Juicy Journeys

Beneath the sun, we stroll along,
Chasing fruits, where we belong.
Coconuts drop with a cheerful thud,
Limes roll past like a slippery dud.

Mangoes wink from the tree above,
While pineapples gossip of sweet love.
We trip and slip on a passion fruit,
Laughing hard in our fruity pursuit.

The Garden of Delights

In this garden, it's a fruit parade,
Watermelons dance, they're unafraid.
Bananas giggle in a bunchy heap,
Avocados look on, dreaming of sleep.

A papaya sings, it's quite the show,
As guavas jive, putting on a glow.
Here every fruit has a tale to share,
With juicy laughter floating in the air.

Flavors of the Infinite Blue

Blueberries swim in the ocean bright,
Doing the backstroke, what a sight!
Pineapples sail on waves of cream,
While kiwis plot a fruity dream.

Strawberries surf on jelly tides,
Coconut boats where sweetness rides.
With every wave, a new nibble found,
Bursting flavors all around.

Waves of Savor

The ocean sings with zest and flair,
Where juicy secrets hide in air.
Lemons laugh, their zest on a spree,
Mimicking waves, so wild and free.

Cherries bounce like beach balls bright,
As oranges roll in the golden light.
Here every splash is a fruity cheer,
Riding the waves, we have no fear!

Sugar and Sizzle

In a pot, the sugar danced,
While the pan did a sizzle prance.
Coconut smiles from the side,
As mango takes a fiery ride.

Pineapple wearing shades so bright,
Says, "Who needs a fancy bite?"
But when the heat starts to rise,
Even limes can't hide their surprise.

Citrus Cascade

Lemons rolling down the hill,
With oranges chasing for the thrill.
Limes giggle in a tangy race,
Tasting joy with every embrace.

Juicy jokes and a zestful cheer,
Swirling fruits bring laughter near.
When grapefruit trips and falls,
All the peels break out in calls.

The Banquet of the Sea

Shrimp in bow ties doing the cha-cha,
While crabs juggle shells like a mantra.
Octopus serves with eight fancy hands,
While seaweed sits with style at the stands.

Clams crack jokes, causing a stir,
And the fish wear hats made of fur.
As waves crash, the laughter grows,
In the banquet where joy overflows.

Enchanted Fruit Tapestry

Berries weave tales of sweet delight,
While cherries dance beneath the moonlight.
Grapes giggle, rolling down the lane,
Creating a tapestry that's never plain.

Kiwi tells secrets, juicy and bold,
To melons who shimmer like fabric of gold.
Together they craft a party so grand,
With laughter and flavors, all perfectly planned.

Caribbean Compote

In a pot, fruits dance and sway,
Pineapples giggle, making play.
Mangoes whisper silly jokes,
As coconuts laugh at clumsy folks.

Bananas slip on beachy sand,
Papayas grin, take a stand.
A juicy feast, oh what a sight,
With a splash of lime, we take flight!

Orchard in the Sky

Up among the clouds so high,
Fruits are bouncing, oh my, oh my!
Peaches juggling in the air,
While cherries play tag without a care.

Bananas swing from fluffy trees,
Lemonade rain brings buzzing bees.
In this orchard, laughs collide,
As funny fruits take us for a ride!

Harvest Moon Bliss

Underneath the gleaming moon,
Fruits unite, they croon a tune.
An apple wearing shades of fun,
Dances 'round till night is done.

Berries twirl in grapevine shoes,
While oranges share their quirky news.
With every bite, giggles abound,
In this paradise, joy is found!

Secrets of the Shoreline

At the beach, fruits hide and play,
Kiwis building castles in the spray.
A coconut tries to surf the waves,
While limes giggle in their caves.

Mangoes searching for a snack,
Found maraschinos with a knack.
With every wave, a silly splash,
Fruit friends unite in a friendly clash!

Sweet Island Lullaby

In the hammock swinging low,
Coconuts fall like a show,
Lizards dance on the sand,
While I munch with one hand.

Pineapple hats, what a sight,
Mangoes rolling in delight,
Singing to the palm tree band,
Banana peels, a slippery land.

With coconut juice in my cup,
I try hard not to trip up,
Squawking birds join the fun,
Making sure I weigh a ton.

So much fruit, I can't complain,
A sticky joy, but who's to blame?
In this island lullaby,
Laughter echoes with the sky.

Radiance of Ripe

Fruits a-glow in morning's light,
Juggling melons feels just right,
Avocados in a race,
Guava smiles on every face.

Berries laugh in vibrant hues,
As citrus starts to spread the news,
Peaches share a juicy wink,
Time for juice, a fruity drink!

Passionfruit takes the cake,
With every poke, it's bound to break,
But don't you dare let it spill,
Pouring joy is quite the thrill!

In this riot of ripe delight,
Silly snacks fill up the night,
With every munch, we gain a cheer,
Radiance spreads, no room for fear!

Spice Route Adventures

On a boat with spice in tow,
I found a curry crab named Joe,
He told me tales of zingy zest,
Waving peppercorns like a jest.

Ginger jumps like a pep rally,
Chilis dance down the alley,
Cinnamon with a twirl and spin,
All join in as we begin!

Nutmeg started a funny fight,
Cloves complained 'bout the fright,
Anise sparked a giggling spree,
All the spices danced with glee!

From each corner scents collide,
A fragrant joke from every side,
In spice route's wacky domain,
Laughter brews like sweet champagne.

The Blissful Harvest

Harvest moon, a sight to behold,
Carrots dancing, brave and bold,
Tomatoes blushing in the sun,
While lettuce twirls, oh what fun!

Potatoes play hide and seek,
Squash with a humorous streak,
Radishes giggle under the ground,
As nature's humor spins around.

Grains are marching in a line,
Wheat grins with a golden shine,
Pumpkins roll with festive cheer,
Telling jokes to everyone near.

In this harvest, joy's the theme,
Every veggie joins the dream,
With baskets full, we laugh and play,
A blissful feast at the end of the day.

Lush Garden Banquet

In a garden where fruits giggle,
Bananas dance, and limes do wiggle.
A party of colors in every slice,
Watermelon winks, oh so nice!

Pomelo wears its hat so sly,
Coconuts whisper, oh my, oh my!
Tomatoes chuckle in their red,
While peppers joke, 'Guess who's well-fed!'

The Singing Pineapple

A pineapple strummed a tune so sweet,
Singing songs with jiggly feet.
Mangoes swayed to the rhythmic beat,
While oranges clapped with juicy heat.

Papaya joined with a voice so bold,
In juicy harmony, a sight to behold.
Coconuts tapped in playful cheer,
As laughter rang from far and near.

Zest and Zing

Lemons threw a zesty bash,
Limes zipped in with a happy flash.
Grapefruits rolled with a cheerful cheer,
While apples laughed, 'We're all here!'

Cherries twirled in a red parade,
Peaches giggled in the sunshine glade.
With every bite, a burst of fun,
This fruity frolic had just begun.

Bounty of the Shore

Mussels are dancing in the sand,
Crabs wearing sunglasses look so grand.
Seashells chuckle, a bubbly crew,
Celebrating flavors from ocean's blue.

Seaweed sways with a salty grin,
While fish dive down, let the feast begin!
With every wave, a giggle or two,
Nature's laughter, fresh and true.

The Blissful Blend

In a coconut hat, I swayed all day,
With a pineapple drink, I giggled away.
Fruits throw a party, it's quite the scene,
Mangoes and guavas, a tropical dream.

But then came the papaya, wobbly and grand,
It slipped from my grip, oh, what a demand!
Splashing in juice, a fruity ballet,
Dancing with mango in a zesty display.

My blender's a wizard, casting a spell,
Whirling and twirling, oh, can you tell?
Banana peels slip, they laugh and they twine,
While limes take a tumble, it's all quite divine!

So here's to the fruits, with their silly embrace,
Delivering laughter with every sweet taste.
The joy of the blend, oh, it never gets old,
In a world of flavors, I'm bold and I'm gold.

Ocean Breeze Bubbles

Under the sun, where the sea meets the shore,
Coconut waves are knocking at the door.
I sip on my drink, while the crabs tap dance,
Trying to catch a wave, giving life a chance.

A jellyfish floats in a fizzy delight,
With bubbles and laughter, it's quite the sight.
Flipping on waves, the sea turtles grin,
While squids join the fun, swirling in sin.

But watch out for seagulls, they swoop and they swipe,
Stealing my taco, oh, that feathered type!
With chortles and hoots, I toss them a fry,
They cackle and dive, oh, my oh my!

As the sunset spills colors, the beach becomes bold,
Where sand meets a splash, and stories unfold.
So come join the laughter, let worries all float,
In the bubbly embrace, we'll share every note.

Flavorful Footprints

Barefoot and sandy, I roam through the land,
Each step leaves a flavor, oh, isn't it grand?
Mango mush squishes between toes with glee,
While cherries pop loudly, oh me, oh my me!

I step on a lemon, the sourness bites,
But giggles in citrus make everything right.
Jellybeans bounce as I skip on my way,
A rainbow of flavors, brightening my day!

Pineapples crown me as the king of this place,
With watermelon wonders, I'm a fruity ace.
Each footprint a story, from beach to the dock,
In this land of delights, oh, tick-tock, tick-tock!

So munch on adventures, let flavors ignite,
With laughter and joy, we savor the night.
Join in the fun, let your taste buds explore,
In the footprints of flavor, who could ask for more?

The Melon Mosaic

In a patch of green, with a grin so wide,
Watermelons play hide and seek, side by side.
Cantaloupes giggle, when they're not in pie,
Honeydews whisper, 'Come on, give it a try!'

Pineapples wear crowns, so regal and neat,
Bouncing on the beach, they dance with their feet.
Kiwi dons shades, oh what a sight to see,
Sipping coconut water, wild and free!

Bananas in pajamas, on swings swinging high,
Mangoes shriek with laughter as they zoom by.
Peaches join the party, all fuzzy and bright,
In this fruity fiesta, they party all night!

Juggling with papayas, what a messy affair,
Caught in a splash, but they don't seem to care.
An orange does a limbo, all zesty and bold,
In this fruity jive, stories unfold!

Tropical Oasis Secrets

A parrot squawks loudly, it's fruit salad time,
Mango salsa dancing, oh isn't it prime?
Limes roll on the sand, saying 'let's have a game',
While cherries wear hats, oh what a sweet claim!

Coconuts giggle as they tumble and roll,
In the shade of palm trees, they lounge on the whole.
Ripe bananas whisper, 'We're Mr. and Mrs.',
Sharing their secrets with giggles and kisses!

Pineapple piñata swings with a chuckle,
Bursting with juice, oh that fruity shuffle!
Papayas do cartwheels, shocking the crowd,
Proving sweet and funny, they're fruity and loud!

At sunset, the fruits form a hilarious line,
Joking and laughing, they sip on divine.
Each slice tells a tale of joy and delight,
In this fruity oasis, everything feels right!

Exotic Fruit Fantasia

In the land of flavors, where laughter's the key,
Durian sings opera, quite pungent and free.
Guava goes surfing, catching waves on a whim,
While starfruit juggles, their edges so slim!

Rambutan's hairdo is wild and quite bold,
It shares fruity gossip, bright stories untold.
Soursop's in the corner, with sour that's sweet,
While pitaya is dreaming of dancing on feet!

Cacao plays guitar, serenading the crowd,
With beans full of magic, sweet laughter allowed.
Passionfruit tosses, a game without rules,
In this fruity fantasia, we're all just good fools!

As night falls upon this zesty delight,
The fruits raise a toast, to laughter so bright.
Each bite is a chuckle, a slice of pure fun,
In this exotic world, we've only begun!

Island Breeze Bites

On an island so sunny, fruits blend and swirl,
Limes spin like tops, causing quite the whirl.
Nuts chatter away, cracking jokes in the shade,
While juicy delights join in the escapade!

Watermelon winks, seducing with charm,
Coconut giggles, sending off a warm balm.
Mangoes sneak peeks, over the rim of their bliss,
Sharing sweet nibbles with a slippery kiss!

Bananas slip-slide in their peel-tastic dance,
Avocados play coy, keeping fruit in a trance.
Pineapple prances with a smile on its crown,
All flavors unite, in this fruity town!

As the sun sets low, they gather in cheer,
Fruit salad commotion brings everyone near.
With laughter and joy, they share every bite,
In the breezy island, everything feels right!

Zesty Zephyr

A breeze that tickles like a feather,
Limes dance with lemons in joyful tether.
Papayas giggle, the pineapples grin,
While coconuts chuckle, 'Let's begin!'

Mango swings on a branch so high,
Winks at the sun, then dares to fly.
Bananas slip with a playful cheer,
'Catch me if you can!' they call from here.

Oranges bounce like a basketball game,
All fruits are laughing, none are the same.
Limeade rivers bubble, frothy and sweet,
As cherries prance on their little feet.

Grapefruit's jokes can be quite absurd,
They talk to the nuts; oh, such a herd!
Lemons and limes, they scream and shout,
In this fruity land, there's no doubt!

The Aroma of Adventure

In a kitchen of curdled chaos and spice,
There lives a ginger with a voice that's nice.
Garlic shimmies on the countertop stage,
While onions cry, 'Oh, what a rage!'

The cinnamon twists like a wiggly snake,
Nutmeg giggles, 'For goodness' sake!'
Saffron struts with a regal air,
Saying, 'I'm fancy, but do I care?'

Pepper shouts, 'Spice it up, dear friends!'
While sage rolls its eyes, laughing, it bends.
A stir in the pot, laughter erupts,
As thyme gives a wink, 'I've got more cups!'

Adventure brews in a bubbling stew,
With all of these flavors, who knows what's new?
Through kitchen antics, we're all in a trance,
Join the spice party, come take a chance!

Mystic Mango Tales

Once upon a time, in a fruit-filled land,
Mangoes hatched jokes never planned.
With a twist of a peel, they'd slip on their grin,
Saying, 'Life's sweeter with a little spin!'

A wise old coconut watched from the tree,
'Watch your step, my dear; it's slippery, see?'
Mangoes giggled and raced down the hill,
'Catch me if you can!' igniting a thrill.

A smoothie parade marched down the street,
Strawberries led with their marching beat.
Limes played trumpets, lemons clanged pots,
While kiwis and berries cheered all the tots.

Under the sun, they danced with delight,
Creating concoctions that sparkled so bright.
In the land of the fruit, where laughter prevails,
Mangoes spin tales with their sweet, sunny trails!

Coconuts and Currents

Coconuts wander on the shoreline's edge,
Waving their palms at the oceanic hedge.
'The water's nice, let's go for a splash!'
Said one to the other, causing a crash!

The waves giggled back, causing a ruckus,
While seashells sang tunes, oh, how they chuck us!
A jellyfish jived with a swishy swirl,
While crabs did the rumba, giving a twirl.

Palm trees rejoiced as the currents rolled,
Their laughter echoed, a sight to behold.
Each coconut chuckled with salty glee,
'Who thought the sea could be this carefree?'

An island of fun where the tides all play,
With coconuts laughing at the break of day.
So bring on the waves and let's have a ball,
In this silly spot, we'll have a grand sprawl!

Sunkissed Delicacies

Sipping drinks in bright colors,
Straws like wild worms in the sun.
Mango giggles with a punch,
While coconuts just want to run.

Pineapples wear hats made of shades,
While bananas break out in dance.
Fruit parties with wacky parades,
Absurd flavors get lost in romance.

The laughter bounces off the skies,
As guavas flaunt their soft embrace.
A fruity war, who's got the prize?
In this cacophony of taste!

So grab your forks, let's make a mess,
Our plates piled high with cheer.
In the sun, we feel so blessed,
Laughing loud, drinking up our beer!

Waves of Flavor

Surfing waves of fruity bliss,
Coconuts splash with pure finesse.
Lemons join in for a twisty ride,
While the cake waves hello, wide-eyed!

Pineapple surfers catch a break,
Riding high on whipped cream lakes.
Peach slices hanging ten on treats,
In this paradise, oh what a feat!

Tangerines toss like beach balls bright,
While jellybeans drift in the night.
Under moonlight, we savor each bite,
Waves of flavors keeping us tight.

So let's toast to this fruity sea,
With flavors that tickle and tease.
Grab your surfboard, come dance with me,
In this joyful fruit-filled breeze!

Lush Garden Melodies

In the garden where flavors bloom,
Carrots sing with a goofy tune.
Celery dancing with glee in the air,
Radishes wearing a silly hair!

Tomatoes blush with a bashful grin,
As lettuce spins like it's in a spin.
Beets boast of their berry red,
While herbs exchange secrets in their bed.

Zucchini juggle in a veggie craze,
While broccoli cuddles in misty haze.
Nature's laughter fills the space,
Every bite's a hearty embrace.

So join this merry garden scene,
Where flavors frolic and guffaws glean.
Nature's whimsies reign supreme,
In this lush patch of dreams!

Citrus Delight

Zesty lemons play on the swing,
While orange slices start to sing.
Limes are tossing confetti high,
As grapefruits giggle, oh me, oh my!

Dancing limes form a jolly crew,
While tangy scents make us woo.
Margaritas flow in vibrant streams,
Reviving childhood, or so it seems.

With every sip, we twist and shout,
Sour faces turn inside-out.
Peeling laughter, zest in the air,
We dive into flavors without a care.

So grab your zest and shake it right,
Join the party, oh what a sight!
Citrus fun, a pure delight,
In this fruity world, love ignites!

The Mango Mirage

Once I found a mango, bright and bold,
Thought it was a treasure, or so I was told.
I took a bite, oh what a surprise,
It was just a peach in disguise!

Sipping smoothies with a twist of lime,
I added too much, what a funny crime.
My blender could not handle the thrill,
It erupted like a fruit-filled hill!

Beneath the palm, I danced with glee,
A coconut fell, right onto me.
I wore it like a crown, quite absurd,
Cheers to my new style, oh how I've stirred!

In the shade of a tree, I took a rest,
A squirrel stole my snack, I must confess.
He smiled at me, a cheeky little mate,
Guess he thought my mangoes were up for debate!

Island Spice Reverie

In the market, spices in a heap,
I sniffed them all, and lost my sleep.
Curry, cumin, and a dash of sass,
I sneezed so loud, folks thought I passed!

With hot sauce drizzled on my plate,
I thought I'd try it, wouldn't that be great?
But my tongue danced like a hula flame,
Next time I'll just stick with mild, who's to blame!

A plate of fish caught my hungry eye,
Was it grilled or was it a pie?
I took a bite, and oh what a pine,
Fish should not taste like dessert, I whine!

In the kitchen, friends all around,
We tried to cook but chaos was found.
Flour in my hair, oh what a sight,
The island kitchen — a wild delight!

Lush Lagoon Dreams

At dusk by the lagoon, I found my fate,
Dreaming of coconut, I just couldn't wait.
I reached for the fruit, it slipped right through,
Splashed in the water, oh what a view!

Floating on leaves, I tried to recline,
But a frog jumped up and said, 'This is mine!'
We argued a bit, who would get the spot,
In the end, we shared, but I got the knot!

A parrot squawked, 'Time to eat, my friend!'
I tossed him a chocolate, thought it would blend.
He looked quite puzzled, then flew away,
Guess he's not a fan of cocoa sorbet!

With friends all laughing, we made a toast,
To the laughter and joy we love the most.
In the lush lagoon, we found our bliss,
With silly antics and such a tasty kiss!

Pineapple Whisper

A pineapple spoke in the kitchen bright,
'Cut me open, I'm a sweet delight!'
But when I sliced it, oh what a roar,
The juice squirted out — a fruity encore!

I tried to bake a pineapple pie,
It turned into mush, oh my oh my!
A recipe gone wrong, but what the heck,
We gobbled it up, a gooey wreck!

Editing cocktails with a twist of fun,
I added too much, now who's on the run?
With umbrellas flying and laughter around,
Our party turned wild, with no one to be found!

Under the sun, we danced with flair,
Pineapples rolled, without a care.
A fruit dance-off, with giggles and leaps,
Oh, how we laughed, in our fruity heaps!

The Sweet Escape

In a land where pineapples dance,
And monkeys in sunglasses enhance,
Coconuts fall, quite uncouth,
As mangoes giggle, oh, what a truth!

A toucan tried to wear a hat,
While a lizard just sat, and sat,
Bananas slip on their own peel,
Squeals of joy are hard to conceal!

Sipping smoothies with a side of fun,
Sunshine makes everyone run,
A hammock sways, laughter rings,
Here, even the parrot sings!

So grab a drink, don't be late,
In this crazy, fruity fate,
With every bite and every smile,
Life's a party all the while!

Harvest of the Tropics

In fields of colors bright and bold,
The vegetables here never feel old,
Papayas giggle as they roll,
While carrots plot to take control!

The tomatoes dance on the vine,
Salsa parties—oh, so divine!
A chili pepper wears a crown,
Wants to be king, not just a noun!

Coconuts peek from their tree beds,
While beets wear hats made of threads,
The harvest festival's a riot,
Even the veggies can't keep quiet!

As baskets fill with humorous treats,
The laughter around is a feast,
Join the fun, don't say no,
In this garden, joy will grow!

Rhythms of Ripe

In a world where fruits sing in tune,
The oranges dance to the light of the moon,
Berries bounce with a mischievous flair,
Throwing their seeds through the warm air!

Pineapples strut down the main street,
With moves that'll knock off your feet,
Mangoes are jamming, what a sight,
Their parties last deep into night!

Lemon drops roll in a playful game,
Trying to none of them be the same,
While guavas laugh, causing a scene,
"Join the groove!" they cheer with a gleam!

So let's shimmy, shake, and twirl,
In this land of fruity whirl,
Every bite brings a giggle and chime,
Here, it's always a good time!

Guava Glow

Under the sun, the guavas gleam,
With colors so bright, they'll make you beam,
Kiwi tries to imitate, but fails,
While the others cheer with fruity tales!

A cricket enviously plays its part,
As a coconut cracks with a hearty start,
Delicious aromas swirl in the air,
Making even the grumpiest share!

The smoothie blender's a rock star now,
Mixing up flavors—a cheeky vow,
With every sip, a giggle erupts,
As fruity madness fully corrupts!

So come on down to this sunny place,
Where fruit and laughter interlace,
In a world that's both sweet and bright,
With guavas glowing, it feels just right!

Nectar of the Tropics

In a land where pineapples dance,
I tripped on a mango in my pants.
The juice splashed up, what a sight,
I chuckled hard, what pure delight.

Coconuts roll down the hill,
My friend yelled, 'Catch that one, will!'
It cracked me up, oh what a scene,
As we slipped on grass, trying to glean.

Bananas wear silly hats too,
They giggle and wave, 'Hello, how do?'
This fruity party, a riot, you see,
A carnival of laughter, just let it be!

So raise your cups, let spirits fly,
With juice that's zany, oh me, oh my!
In this giggling garden, we'll forever stay,
Sipping on sunshine, come what may.

Chocolate and Coconuts

In the land of cocoa dreams,
A monkey yells, 'Pass the creams!'
He slipped on chocolate, oh what a fuss,
We laughed so hard, made quite the cuss.

Coconuts bounced like a beach ball,
Each one looked ready to have a ball!
I tried to juggle, went quite awry,
Landed on my head, and oh, my oh my!

Beneath the palm trees, cocoa breeze,
A bird snatched my treat, with such ease.
I jumped and twirled, called for a truce,
But all I got back was a cheeky excuse!

So let's blend the nuts and the sweet,
A smoothie of giggles, a tasty treat.
With a sprinkle of laughter and a dollop of cheer,
We'll sip on joy, year after year.

The Sweetness of Sunshine

Oh, the sun shines bright on this delightful spree,
Where lollipops hum and dance with glee.
A group of strawberries sport funny hats,
They twirled in the breeze, like chubby acrobats.

Papayas play hide and seek, oh so sly,
When I found one, it whispered, 'Why, oh why?'
With giggles and wiggles, it leapt from my hand,
Landing in pudding, oh isn't that grand?

Pineapples chuckle, in bright shades of gold,
Telling tales of adventures, ancient and bold.
They wink and they nudge, 'Join in the fun,'
And I rolled with laughter, under the sun.

So let's raise a toast, with a fizzy punch,
To all the sweet fruit that makes us munch.
With sunshine and joy, our hearts will sing,
In a world where laughter is the favorite fling.

Jungle Juice Journey

On a slippery vine, I took my first step,
With wild creatures telling me to prep.
A parrot squawked, 'Mix juice with flair!'
While I fumbled with fruit, spilling everywhere.

'What's the secret?' I asked a sly snake,
He winked and replied, 'Just shake, shake, shake!'
In a blender of chaos, I found my groove,
With berries dancing, ready to move.

Lemons danced jitterbug, limes did the twist,
While I tried to measure, a fruity mist.
Suddenly, a gorilla took my hat,
I shouted, 'Hey dude, that hat's where it's at!'

But we blended together, the wild and sweet,
Creating a potion, quite the treat.
With cheers and laughter, we raised our cups high,
A jungle juice journey, oh my, oh my!

Papaya Paradise

In a land where papayas grow,
Laughter dances, breezes blow.
A fruit so splendid, soft and sweet,
It winks at you with every treat.

Banana peels slip, oh what a sight,
Everyone's laughing, what a delight!
With a spoonful of yogurt, oh so creamy,
Who knew a fruit could be this dreamy?

The sun shines bright, like a yellow smile,
Join the feast, stay for a while.
Under palm trees, we giggle and play,
In our papaya paradise, we're never gray!

Coconut Currents

Coconuts fall, thump on the ground,
Next thing you know, you're rolling around.
With a cracked shell, a milk cascade,
A coconut joke? Well, here's one made!

The coconut shy at the fair so bright,
Aim for the targets, but don't lose your sight.
Splashing coconut water, it's quite a scene,
Turns out that fruit's a slippery queen!

With every sip, a chuckle to share,
More like a doozy with every dare.
In coconut currents, we drift and laugh,
Creating memories, our joyful path!

A Symphony of Sorbet

A scoop of mango, a twist of lime,
Singing sweetly, oh, what a rhyme.
Each little flavor leaps like a frog,
Wobbly cones? They dance in a bog!

Berry blasts and slushy tracks,
Watch out for drips, don't wear them like slacks!
It's a carnival in each frozen bite,
With every taste, our giggles take flight.

Beneath the sun, with spoons held high,
Melting moments, oh my, oh my!
In our symphony of sorbet delight,
Every scoop's a tune, everything's right!

Sunset Citrus

Lemonade rivers and citrus skies,
Sipping sunshine, what a surprise!
Juggling oranges, the moment's ablaze,
A zesty burst that'll brighten your days.

With grapefruits winking, oh what a tease,
Pineapple hats dancing in the breeze.
Lime slices laugh, such a vibrant crew,
Splashing zest on everyone, too!

Sunset whispers in colors, a feast,
Twirling fruit salads, let's be a beast.
With every slice, a giggle unfolds,
In this citrus wonder, joy never gets old!

The Flavorful Horizon

In a world where pineapples dance,
Coconuts roll in a curious trance.
Mangoes giggle, juicy and bright,
While bananas wear sunglasses, oh what a sight!

Swirling drinks in coconuts come,
Chanting, 'Taste me—you won't feel glum!'
Papaya polka steps on the shore,
As lime wedges beg for just one more!

Fruit-flavored hats with tiny umbrellas,
Wear 'em at parties, they'll make you the fella!
Grapefruits gossip, sharing their zest,
While tourists joke about the fruitiest fest!

At sunset, mango margaritas flow,
Making the beach the best show in town!
Laughter and flavors mix with delight,
As the horizon bursts, a comedic sight!

Vivid Island Infusion

Kiwi kids on the sandy spree,
Wrestling oats in a fruity sea.
Strawberries in hats, how silly they stand,
While oranges juggle with a beach ball in hand!

Palm trees sway to the rhythm of pies,
And guavas burst out in perfect disguise.
Pineapples sing in a campy tune,
As sweet limes dance underneath the moon!

Smoothies with giggles, what can go wrong?
Chasing watermelons, the ultimate song!
Papayas and peaches throw a big bash,
Where laughter and flavors make quite the splash!

In this land of zesty, bright, and fun,
Where every fruit bursts with a smile, not a pun!
Join in the frolic, embrace the cheer,
For every sip brings the island near!

Sips of Serenity

Lemonade rivers where the laughter flows,
Watermelon boats with giggles that glow.
As chill coconuts whisper secrets in shade,
Pineapples giggle—'Just take a lemonade!'

A beach full of flavors, so wild and bright,
Strawberries tickle as night meets light.
Sipping sweet nectar from glasses that wink,
Lime slices banter, 'Come join the pink drink!'

Floating on waves with silly delight,
Berries bounce up, a whimsical flight.
Bananas in flip-flops, oh what a sight!
Each sip brings laughter, a whimsical bite!

Under the sun, where time takes a pause,
Every fruit plays and breaks all the laws.
So grab a glass, let the fun cascade,
In a land where flavors bring joy unmade!

Colorful Fruit Jubilee

Cherry fireworks light up the sky,
As fruits in wigs dance, oh my, oh my!
Kiwis on stilts, prancing about,
While passion fruits shout, 'Join in our rout!'

A festival of sips, not a frown in sight,
Lettuces dance under twinkling light.
Jubilant juicers spin a tune,
While cherries do cha-chas, oh sweet monsoon!

In this world where fruits wear their crowns,
Bananas breakdance, icing browns.
Popsicles joke, tossing cools with flair,
As hilarious fruits fill the jubilant air!

So gather your friends, let the colors collide,
Laughing with flavors, life's joyous ride.
In a playful blend of fruity delight,
Every jubilee brightens the night!

Island Whispers

On the shore, the palm trees sway,
While parrots laugh and play.
A crab wears shades, struts with pride,
As beach balls bounce, and tides collide.

The sea turtle tells me jokes,
While fish in bowties giggle and poke.
A piña colada spills with a laugh,
As we chase seagulls, our chubby craft.

In the sand, we build a throne,
A fortress of shells, tall and prone.
But watch out for that sneaky tide,
It loves a game of hide and slide!

So let's dance barefoot, let the fun rise,
Underneath the zany skies.
With every whisper of the breeze,
Comes a chuckle from the coconut trees.

Mango Sunsets

As the sun dips low, colors blend,
A splash of mango, summer's friend.
The sky's a canvas, wild and bright,
A fruit salad feast, what a sight!

Beneath the palm, we sip our juice,
With laughter bubbling, we let loose.
A parrot mimics our silly shouts,
While monkey friends swing in and out.

Sunglasses on, we're the life of the show,
Dancing with shadows, stealing the glow.
Kiwi friends joining in with their charm,
We hoot and holler, what's the harm?

And as the last light fades away,
We'll reminisce on this funny play.
With mango mustaches, we close our day,
And dream of sunrises at the bay.

Coconut Dreams

Coconuts plop, a thud on the shore,
One rolls away—now who wants more?
With laughter we gather, the prize of the day,
Each sip is a giggle, oh what a play!

A pirate hat on my coconut friend,
With a swashbuckling smile that won't end.
Rum punch swirls in a hula dance,
As we shake our hips, lost in the trance.

In coconut dreams, we surf the waves,
In our silly hats, we're all so brave.
An octopus juggles our fruity delight,
As we cheer him on, what a funny sight!

With every sip, our giggles abound,
In this nutty paradise, joy is found.
As night blankets all in a starry beam,
We flip-flop home, lost in our dream.

Spice of the Ocean

A pinch of salt in the ocean breeze,
Bringing spice, just like a tease.
Rainbow fish dance in a saucy regale,
Telling tales of their salty trail.

The cook makes a stew with a wink and a grin,
As crabs near the fire invite their kin.
With seaweed wraps and jokes galore,
The dinner table's never a bore.

Lobsters in tuxedos, oh what a sight,
Doing the cha-cha in the moonlight.
With every chop and every slice,
The ocean's laughter, oh so nice!

So gather 'round, let's share the cheer,
The spice of the ocean brings joy near.
With every bite and every jest,
In this seaside feast, we find our zest!

www.ingramcontent.com/pod-product-compliance
Lightning Source LLC
Chambersburg PA
CBHW062109280426
43661CB00086B/377